Sockemus Theifus

by Lawanda Madison

Illustrated by Jacolyn Wingo

Sockemus Thiefus

I had the sweetest, baby girl,
She was like the perfect song,
Time seemed to fly by so fast,
And suddenly, things started to go wrong.

She had her own clothing,
Of course, I had mine too,
But, in no time at all,
We were wearing the same sized shoe.

Things were still fine,
We switched shoes around the clock,
But, after washing loads of clothes,
I was always missing a sock.

I know that this is common in households,
I was always on a mission,
To find and match every sock,
But, this is not what I envisioned.

The socks that were missing a match,
I placed in a bag in my sock drawer,
However, to my dismay,
My sock bag seemed to grow more and more.

I had numerous socks that were missing its match,
I was down to six pair in all,
My daughter always removed the clothes from the dryer,
I guess this was my downfall.

It frustrated me that my socks were missing,
I wondered when this would end,
When friends came to visit,
A sock would go home with her friend.

I contacted her friend's mother,
She stated that it was happening to her too,
Her daughter had taken all of her socks,
And she didn't know what to do.

We continued discussing the issue,
Then, we came up with a plan,
If we wrote our initial on each sock,
They wouldn't take our socks again.

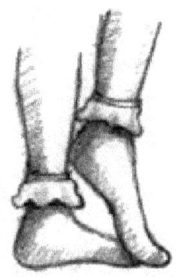

I decided to check her room,
Under her bed, there was a box,
I opened it, and to my surprise,
There were all of my missing socks.

I gathered each sock from the box,
And matched it with the other,
I left the empty box on her bed,
So that she'd know I'd blown her cover.

As she returned home from her friend's,
She was as content as she could be,
Until she saw the empty box,
She seemed so upset with me.

As if she had been betrayed,
By someone she truly confided in,
At the time, wearing mismatched socks
Had become the new trend.

She'd wear different colors to match her shirt,
Sometimes, she'd match them with her pants,
Her drawer had an abundant amount of socks,
So, I had to take a stance.

I wanted to wear my own socks,
And to make this official,
On the bottom of each of my socks,
I added my initial.

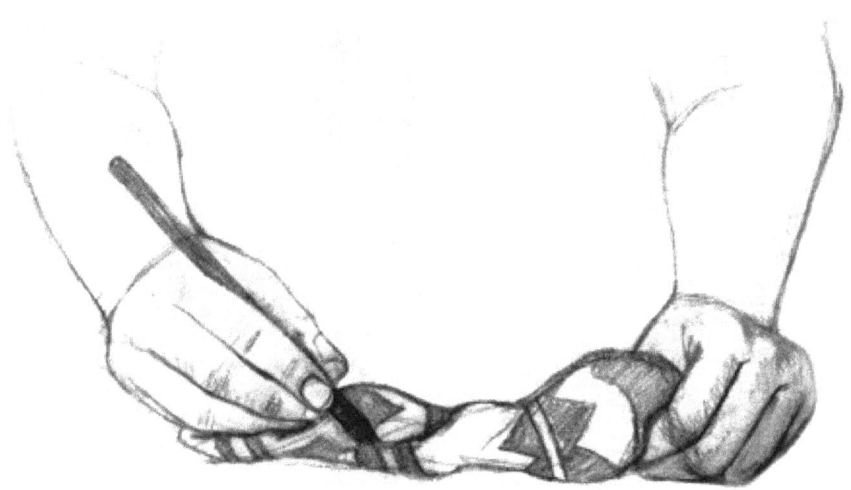

I used a permanent marker,
Wrote my initial as dark as it could get,
The thought of losing my socks now,
Was something that I fret.

Writing my initial on each sock,
Seemed a little strange,
But, it didn't stop her and her friends
From having their sock exchange.

I decided to take a walk,
With my hands on my hips I stood,
I thought, my initial is going to be
On every kid's sock in my neighborhood.

I took her to our family doctor,
The doctor seemed rather stunned,
She laughed hysterically when I finished my story,
Of her, I was no longer fond.

I called an orthopedic,
Because I thought it was her feet,
After explaining the situation,
With us, the doctor would not meet.

I took her to a psychologist,
It was a waste of my time,
After explaining the issue to him,
He asked if he could examine my mind.

I finally met a doctor,
She was standing in the midst,
She said, "I had a similar situation,
I'll refer you to my clothesthiefologist".

She showed me a picture of her daughter,
Her demeanor became motherly and gentle,
She wiped tears as she spoke of her child,
I wasn't expecting her to get sentimental.

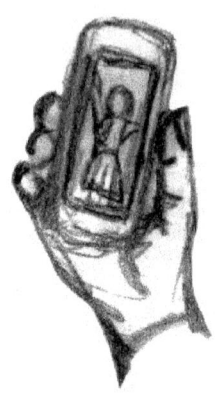

She then spoke about the doctor,
I considered everything she was stating,
I decided to check his website,
And found the doctor had a five star rating.

I researched this doctor thoroughly,
He said he had seen this before,
He'd known all of the symptoms,
With his method, it would happen no more.

At least that's what his website stated,
I'm determined to see,
How he's going to get this under control,
How explicit he will be!

I called and made an appointment,
His office was fifteen minutes away,
I had to work early in the morning,
So, it was set for later in the day.

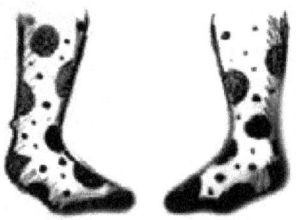

I looked around as we entered his office,
I shook my head in disgrace,
It seemed that many others shared this problem,
As there were people all over the place.

I also noticed that those that were leaving,
Seemed to walk out happily,
As if the doctor fixed all of their problems,
I wondered, "Can he also fix this issue for me?"

I grew more and more anxious each minute,
With the service I was taken aback,
My daughter was taken to a playroom,
Then, the nurse politely hung my coat on a rack.

This doctor could see my frustration,
Even before our session began,
He was informed that we had visited many doctors,
Now, we were trying this again.

I explained the issue to the doctor,
I gave examples as often as I could,
The doctor nodded occasionally as I spoke,
I felt as if I finally found someone that understood.

He walked away for quite some time,
He returned, stating that he was sorry to keep us,
He smiled as he studied his notes,
He said, "Your daughter has Sockemus Theifus".

"Sock-e-ma-what? What is in the world is that?
It sounds more like a crime."
He said, "Your daughter isn't misbehaving,
This issue will weaken with time."

I felt as if he'd failed me,
I grabbed my coat, and headed for the door,
I said, "I thought that you could help me.
Your website stated that it would happen no more."

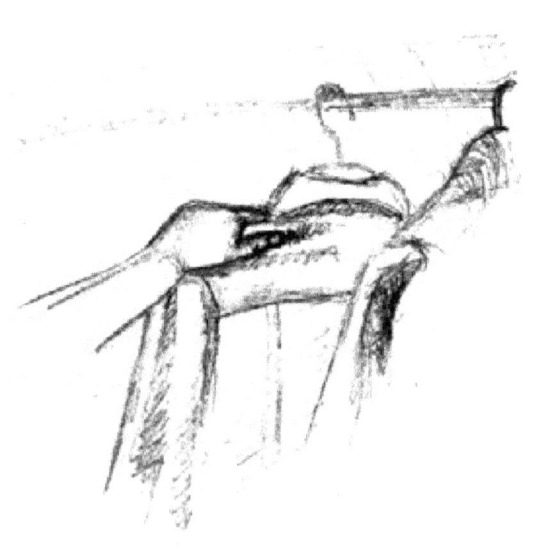

He said, "Ma'am, please listen to me,
Cause what I tell you is true,
She'd never take from anyone,
This situation is about you."

"I know that this seems crazy,
It's leaving you in shock,
You're such an awesome person to her,
With pride, she wears your sock."

"But, in a few years this will end,
The time will go by so fast,
She's going to become a teenager,
This doting sock thing won't last."

"She will make new friends,
Some jock will come and steal her heart,
She'll find an interest in other things,
This love for your socks is sure to part."

"Movies and games will entertain her,
She'll talk to her friends around the clock,
She'll get caught up in her own life,
There will be no time to think of your sock."

"She'll focus more on her classes,
Maybe have an interest in a sport,
Other thoughts are going to consume her,
The thoughts of you will become short."

Maybe I was overreacting,
I kind of figured it from the start,
To think that my child wouldn't think of me
Would surely break my heart.

I absorbed everything he had stated,
Slumped into my chair as he stood tall,
I'd wasted my time seeing numerous doctors,
When there wasn't a problem at all.

I stood and thanked the doctor,
I shook his hand before I left,
I walked down the Hall of Humiliation,
So disappointed in myself.

In the playroom was my daughter,
Her eyes shined so bright for me,
I hugged her with all my might,
The shame on my face, I didn't want her to see.

PARENTS:

When your kids wear your clothing,
Please do not reprimand,
Maybe they just like your style,
Please try to understand.

It was you that purchased the clothes,
That means you liked them too,
It's possible that your kids wear the clothing,
Because they liked how it looked on you.

So, embrace each day with your children,
Be mindful of how you spend it,
My daughter still has Sockemus Theifus,
And I'm enjoying every minute.

From the Author:

This book started as a joke between me and my daughter. Some of the events actually occurred, which increased my desire to finish the writing. At first, the inability to find my socks irked me beyond words. But, after watching her grow up so fast, I began to wonder if those things that bothered me really mattered. I wondered, "When she gets older, will she still take my style into consideration, or will she focus more on the latest trends? Will she continue to spend time with me, or will she spend time with her friends? How much is my life going to change as she gets older?" Often, as I'm about to head to work, she advises that I look nice. I won't get to hear that from her as she heads off to college, or when she moves into her own home. Therefore, I acknowledge each instance as a great memory of time spent with someone that truly loves me. She has been my personal cheerleader through many moments, and I couldn't ask for a better child.

This isn't just a book about socks. It's a book written to acknowledge the extreme measures that some parents take when their children are only being children. So many children have been hurt, tortured, or even killed by the people they admire. Please take these words into consideration. Please stop harming your children.

LaWanda

Photo by André Moore

Lawanda Madison is also
the author of *Exposure* and *Falling Up*.

Jacolyn Wingo,
Illustrator / Graphic Designer and Dreamer
www.jacolynwingo.com

© *All rights reserved. No part of this publication may be reproduced, stored in a retrieval system, or transmitted in any form or by any means, electronic, mechanical, photocopying, recording, or otherwise, without written permission of the publisher.*

www.ingramcontent.com/pod-product-compliance
Lightning Source LLC
Chambersburg PA
CBHW061349040426
42444CB00011B/3158